Parts of the Main

Jane Williams was born in England in 1964 and raised in Australia. Her poems have been widely published and anthologised since the early 1990s. Her first book won the Anne Elder Award. Other awards for her poetry include the Bruce Dawe Prize and the Dinny O'Hearn Fellowship. She has been a guest reader at festivals and poetry venues within Australia, USA, Canada, UK, Ireland, Malaysia, Czech Republic and Slovakia. She lives in Tasmania with her partner Ralph Wessman.

Also by Jane Williams

Poetry
outside temple boundaries
The Last Tourist
Some Towns and other poems
Begging the question
City of Possibilities
Days Like These: new and selected poems 1998–2013

Short stories
Other Lives

Parts of the Main
Jane Williams

Acknowledgements

Australian Poetry Review
Everything About Us Anthology (2016, Kuala Lumpur)
We Society Anthology (2016, New Zealand)
Poetry and Place Anthology (2016, Australia)
Writing to the Wire Anthology (2016, Australia)
Cordite Poetry Review
Muddy River Review
2015 Best Australian Poems
The Australian
Australian Book Review – States of Poetry Anthology
Pedestal Magazine
Eye to the Telescope
2017 Rhysling Anthology
Rattle

'The boy, the duck, the rock' – highly commended
2014 Bruce Dawe Poetry Prize

A selection from this book was shortlisted for the
2015 Whitmore Press Manuscript Prize.

I am grateful to the Copyright Agency (Australia) and the Cultural
association Štúrovo and Vicinity (Slovakia) for a three-month
residency at the Bridge Guard Residential Art/Science Centre,
Štúrovo in Slovakia.

Parts of the Main
ISBN 978 1 76041 385 9
Copyright © text Jane Williams 2017
Cover image by Emily Kelly

First published 2017 by
GINNINDERRA PRESS
PO Box 3461 Port Adelaide 5015 Australia
www.ginninderrapress.com.au

Contents

Bells and Whistles	9
Still/life	11
Everything about us	12
Comfort	13
Renewal	15
Brogue	16
The newlywed	17
There are places	19
Pembantu rumah (maid)	20
Ular sawa (python)	21
Days of blue and banter	22
The ice cream gouger of Prague	24
Prayer for the lads	25
Preamble	26
First morning in Venice	27
Bells and whistles	29
In the ladies restroom	30
Proof of existence	32
From the sidelines	33
Once upon a time spam	34
Plaza Perfect	35
The Memory Machines	37
Unplugged	38
Elsewhere	39
Rosa Villar Jarionca	40
Confessions of a serial eavesdropper	42
Climate control	43
Degrees of separation	44

Parts of the Main — 45

- Doppelgangers — 47
- A personal history of prayer — 48
- This complicated inner life — 49
- The birds — 50
- The body has become its own refrain — 51
- On World Heart Day — 52
- Awakening — 54
- The boy, the rock, the duck — 55
- Co — 57
- Part of the main — 59
- My mother asks me to write a butterfly poem — 60
- Depth of field — 62
- When the last harp maker shuts up shop — 63
- Sister moon — 64
- Fifty — 65
- Dog Beach — 66
- Icebreaker — 68
- Flashback — 70
- Mass at Bass — 71
- The day the earth moved — 73
- Through a barbershop window — 74
- The poet and the pea — 75
- Swallowing the sky — 76
- Show and tell — 77
- I have come to believe — 79
- The Waiting Game — 80
- Superpowers — 81
- Hooked to this — 82

Guarding the Bridge — 85

- Guarding the bridge — 87
- View from the Children's Home — 88
- They called it the gentle revolution — 89
- A mist hangs low — 90
- Maria Valeria Mathilde Amalie — 91
- Tonight the light — 93
- Swans in flight — 94
- Despite our differences or because of them the interview goes well… — 95
- Everything is negotiable — 97
- The bridge stands but the chestnut tree is dying — 98
- In the witching hour — 99
- Days of leaving – notes to self — 100

For Ralph

Bells and Whistles

Still/life

After a drawing by a pregnant woman on Christmas Island, who asked if her baby could be adopted by an Australian family

It could be the same butcher paper I once drew on; bold out of proportion larger than life mostly happy-to-be-here Crayola child drawings. But it's not, is it? It's detention issue paper. And you are not a child. You are with child. And you cannot be happy to be where you cannot be more than this; incarcerated self-portrait with foetus. Pencilled in grey. You draw yourselves into a birdcage. Angle your long hair at a sway. How much time do you spend rocking to sleep? Does your joyless face dream-smile? The umbilical cord reaches up, connecting to your valentine heart. Your unborn baby's speech bubble begs for misspelt help because, like love, help is one of those words we should recognise before we translate, interpret, process. At the bottom of the page the outline of Australia. A cut-out blank. The ignoble space and silence of it. Where your feet disappear. Correction, you have no feet. You have drawn yourself without feet. So we must ask the questions – What happens now? What happens next?

Everything about us

Everything about us makes us strangers here. Out-of-place tourists waking into another Ramadan day. Into a culture we are privy to but not part of. A neighbourhood free from souvenirs, from brochures and itineraries. The taxi driver asks, Why? The memory-making of everyday living elsewhere is a blueprint for home. The call to prayer echoes across tiled rooftops, dipping and rising through alleys and stairwells. Our hosts invite us to celebrate Eid al-Fitr: the sugar feast, the sweet festival. But this morning and for seven days more their first meal of the day must be eaten before sunrise, sate them until sunset. We buy street food from vendors who smile at us curiously. Our cameras become dangerous pets questioning intent; tourists bring back photos, travellers bring back stories. But labels are blankets we hide under, revealing selective truths by torchlight. Empty beer bottles replicate like drones on the laminate bench top, then stop. We moderate. Abstain. Our bodies thank us. A new ethos sidles up to the old one, we let parts of it in – no more or less than we need. Children signal our unbelonging in hand-cupped whispers. The mosque's blue domed minaret, zigzagged with gold is striking as lightning in a cloudless sky. Motorbikes and pedestrians move in practised, haphazard synchronicity, suggesting accidents happen anyway, anywhere. Hijabs form part of the landscape – their colours and patterns individual as dreams. A woman and child cross the road slowly, a small sway over their journey's end. As she bends to his level, the traffic adjusts itself around them. She kisses his left cheek, right cheek, then again – before watching him disappear through the school gates. And this is the familiar. The anchor I hold to. This gesture of loving separation. This unified prayer that all we see in our children will be seen. As we hand them over. As we let them go.

Comfort

Tonight it's Chinese food tweaked
to accommodate a Western palate,
white tablecloths encouraging
at least entry-level table manners,
attentive waiters, warm wet
hand towels, the ocean in a glass tank.
We're out with friends,
swapping travel stories,
listing but not naming animals
we've eaten,
when a neighbouring table
becomes a medical emergency.
Mid-sentence, mid-gesticulation
a woman has stopped.
Stopped talking. Stopped moving.
Her cutlery and crockery,
the perfect mound of rice –
all still lifes now.
Her panoramic vision turned inward.
The voices of family members
beseech strangers to inhabit their titles:
Doctor. Nurse. First aider.
Soon someone is monitoring
pulse and breath, time and tide.
Someone is whispering *mini-stroke*.
While the maître d' discreetly
scans the room for undesirable
ripple effects the rest of us
offer our kindest clichés and grapple:
Looking. Not looking. Eating. Not eating.

Getting on. Getting on.
The woman's husband,
(whose only enemy now is inaction)
phones for the ambulance,
strokes his wife's hair.
Repeats her name over and over
as if it is the last, the very last magic word.
Then he turns.
And we watch as he turns
from mounting anxieties
to the comfort of a single sauce-drenched
spring roll, and this would be darkly funny
if not so familiar
for which of us could deny him
this simple affirmation,
the vivifying sweet and sour of its call.

Renewal

It was before mobile phones and predictive text. Before GPS. They were out walking together and there was a pothole or maybe a crack in the pavement through which the root of a tree had begun its necessary search for water. And one of them tripped (accidentally or on purpose) and the other was jolted. They became distracted, untethered and before they knew what had happened, she turned one way and he the other. They found themselves walking streets peopled with neighbours who did not recognise the him or her of them. It was a strange skin-tingling tightrope walk. They walked through exhilaration to exhaustion. They walked until they each found a resting place; a prayer room or maybe a watering hole. Where she could let her slip slip and he could run his hands through his hair and they could take stock for a moment, embracing their alien beings. Remembering all they hadn't yet shared – old odd things they hadn't thought worthy until now and new startling ones they were on the brink of discovering. They walked on, singly, somehow renewed. And when they turned a certain corner, there they were, more pleased to have been lost and found than they had ever been to simply be together. We must never, they agreed, each catching the breath of the other, we must never stop meeting like this…

Brogue

In my father's country I am
part tourist from down under,
part prodigal daughter.
And all ears.

The singular northern accent
I grew up with now just one
among many variables.
And I fall for them all.

Perhaps we yearn for a melody
the way we yearn for faith
even as we call it something else.

The ear (not the stomach
or even the eye) is the quickest,
surest path to this woman's heart.

It's why I make an art
of eavesdropping.

And why I have no retort
when I overhear the boast –
one busker to another,
Sure the Australians
throw money at you
just for speaking…

The newlywed

opens her umbrella behind me;
another canopy of colour
in a long line tapering toward
the tower and permission
to climb the iron skeleton,

she introduces herself
by declaring
between racking coughs
that she is amazed,
she is amazed by everything.

The embers of her dark eyes
flicker and flame
a shade brighter
than her ruined teeth
as she asks if I
have children, how many?

She has none – not yet, too soon –
*I am new…*she confesses,
smiling a pause before rounding
off in softly accented English
…I am newly wed.

As she speaks her left hand
emerges from the folds
of her honeymoon dress
to flutter across midriff
allowing the glimmer once more
of that tiny wished-upon star.

When her husband returns
from the designated area
for smokers, she whispers
his name that is her name now
and he responds

by taking his place by her side
in the rain in Paris, where,
all things being equal, one love
-fuelled day leads ably to the next.

There are places

It's just cracker night,
still – there are places
you'd rather not be left
wondering, wandering:
hills called
break me neck
and *bust me gall*,
stretches of road
where crows
take their time
with exposed innards
(it doesn't take a quick study
to know this kind of buffet
is perpetual),
where the screech
of black cockatoos
dies down to reveal
the small sonic boom
of gunshot,
where the boogeyman
is real as regret,
and even your best behaviour
might not be good enough
to get you all the way home.

Pembantu rumah (maid)

Each morning of the dry spell she waters the potted plants. Uncoiling the green hose she walks the circumference of the top floor balcony and waters the potted plants. The apartment is large enough for a large family of tourists. But there is just the two of us. I see her through the tinted glass of the kitchen window. I try not to look up from the table. How can I not look up from the table? She is there every morning. I am here every morning. She wears plain dark T-shirts and long pants. On special occasions she wears a long dress of yellow flowers and a headscarf the colour of wet sand. When she smiles involuntarily the gap in her teeth winks like providence. The morning I ask her name, the sun leaks lazily through a portal in the weeks long blanket of grey sky. I point this out as if it were a mirage. Some kind of unwritable postcard. And then it rains…

Ular sawa (python)

A true story our host assures us. A pattern in the grass. A trick of light. A shimmer of heat. Manifest. Before and after photos. Look. The aged tabby, deaf in one ear, a regal stance, perfunctory glance at the camera. How much time lapses? Next photo. See here. A bulge of skin and scale. The reshaped cat-shape. The snake catcher measuring eight feet, his job made easy by an unyielding fence. Caught. Caught out. All of us. These widening highways. These fragmented landscapes. Hunger and thirst. Remember, whisper the urban mythologists, the suburban yarn spinners. Remember the day of the python…

Days of blue and banter

Pushing on through nothing but fresh air –
sometimes that's the hardest thing;
no one to see or hear you but the sheep,
the odd donkey, your perfect baby,
the benign bluestone walls of your house.

A glut of blackberries wasted on you –
but not the green or how the green
undulates until it reaches the wild
blue currents of the Atlantic,
how you long some days to roll with it.

A routine walk
steering your state of the art pram
along narrow unmade roads. Perhaps humming
a tune to placate the son whose inarticulate life
now guides your own. Wild fuchsia nodding
the way. A little blue beneath the twirl.
Is that why we say *Deora Dé*?

A chance meeting with the elderly neighbour.
The usual banter; how grand it is, the weather,
how unseasonally warm. And he smiles
so you smile. How happy and healthy
the babe in the buggy.

And just then something else, something
more – rising unbidden
from the untold depth of you.
A rush of words escaping the myth
of motherhood to settle in that sweet ache
between generation and gender.

When you worry you've said too much,
it's the old man who gently closes the divide;
six sisters who never knew how to speak
to each other or anyone
about anything that mattered.
No blue bright enough to keep them buoyed.
How they're all, each one dead now,
from the cancer. No more to say. *So you talk*,
he implores, *you talk away…*

Wild fuchsia is known in Irish Gaelic as *Deora Dé* – Tears of God

The ice cream gouger of Prague

Ice cream should be happier than this
sullen server demonstrating
what a tough act being civil can be
when rage is chaffing at the bit.

It was if we were asking her to perform
an indecent act right there on the counter.

Oh the way she gouged out
that cappuccino ice cream,
really, gouge is the right word
(I expect she'd be pleased to hear that).

Each small scoop slapdashed
atop thinly crisp cones like
frozen eyeball spoils of war.

Wondering then what kind
of voodoo this might be,
I pictured her enemy; sightless, stumbling,
suddenly, finally, wounded as she.

Unable to trust herself to speak,
it was all she could do not to spit.

I tell you it broke my heart a little –
face like a smacked arse,
mouth set against a world of hurt
so far from the joyful commands
of happy ice cream land.

Prayer for the lads

The lads are carousing
though it's twenty-fourteen
Crying Cockles and Mussels
all the way home.

The moon too in full form
ghosting swans down the river
Alive Alive O
There's no room at the inn

or the refuge for women.
The neighbourhood feels it
this lunar lit night.
Send the lads on their way then

to wear themselves out
through streets broad and narrow,
gentling dreams of the men
they'll wake as tomorrow.

Words in italics taken from the traditional Irish song 'Molly Malone'

Preamble

at the pre-dawn kitchen table reading the kinds of poems that compel me to write the kinds of poems that begin by feeling the poetry in everything. In the first motorbike of the day competing with the drone of the last mosquito of the night. In the whooshing of the air conditioner mimicking waves breaking on the shores of some fantasy island. In the tempting aloofness of that last piece of pie in the fridge. In the barking of neighbourhood dogs sounding so close to conversation I feel like an eavesdropper. In filling the kettle. In recognising the status of props; their usefulness as both distractors and signposts. In the compulsion becoming something else. Becoming me back in bed with you. My head on your chest. Your arm responding without missing a snoring beat. The synthetic bits of us humming along like they've always belonged and who knows maybe they have. My sleeping heart whispering to your sleeping heart. *This is it; the poem I can only ever write the preamble to.*

First morning in Venice

How easy to lose one's point of origin.
The tourist at the next table reminds us
even once around the square
and you could be anyone anywhere;
one minute a temporary lagoon dweller
the next a misplaced fixture in time and space –
implausible spec in the eye of the camera.

She would be lost still, she claims,
were it not for the old man
who led her back…eventually…
through a succession of frescoes,
across a fifteenth-century plaza,
somehow threading three floors
of hospital corridors
long ago inhabited by monks.

In one room they fixed his left leg,
in another his right eye, and there,
part of his heart. Returning him to life
time and again. *Miracolo*.

We listen like children intent on believing,
the walls of the hotel's breakfast room
closing in. We dismiss the guide map,
cold coffee and half-eaten pastries –
hungry for a tale of our own.

Outside: fabled alleys, web of waterways,
arched bridges, rumoured hauntings,
refugee history, the anonymity
of carnival masks – all waiting
to waylay us from whatever task,
whatever path it is we think we're on.

Bells and whistles

aliens en masse at market. Is that who we are here?
And here may as well be Mars. Let's call it Mars then.
See how quickly the line is drawn? How reluctantly

it blurs? From this point forward every word becomes
a retreat of sorts. On Mars at market en masse. A Martian
sitting on wet well-tourist-trodden ground. Trouser-less

legs at an almost perfect right angle. One whole, the other
roughly puckered – sausage-like – at the knee.
If we don't acknowledge matter how can we see beyond it?

Where does this question come from if not from the unlinked
sausage leg of the Martian? This is the beginning
of the guessing game. Animal. Mineral. Vegetable. A catalogue

of names assigned to abstract locations we only ever pass through.
We know the answer is older than the question. Still we advance.
Almost but never quite believing that in the end, if nothing else,

surely all the bells and whistles will save us…

In the ladies restroom

of a pit stop restaurant
between developing cities
I join the usual queue
of women anywhere.

Tourists mostly,
holding bladders at the end
of a six hour bus trip;
choosing willpower
over straddling the bowl
on treacherous roads.

Too tired for talk
we eye the small piece
of pale pink soap
on the cracked white basin
like a depreciating jewel.

Sidestepping two locals
squat on the floor
one behind the other,
we register the bare
expanse of back,
the hand applying salve,
three dark pink welts
each the width
of a trouser belt.

We are extraneous yet part
of this public private space,
this force field
of ministrations
where sound has no place
        except

in the visceral,
the contraction
of blood vessels,
the redirected breath,
the body's primordial
next careful move.

Proof of existence

I wake with Garbo, wanting to be alone; it's that kind of morning, the mold on my to-do list outgrowing whatever small purpose I had given myself, then failed to believe in, and now I want all the possibilities, all the privileges of this spring day to myself – whatever hidden truths a walk in the park might reveal, loosed from the obligations, the diversions of technology and time. I take the delirious risk of leaving my phone at home, and soon my mind is drifting then spinning past identity, past the timesharing of invested relationships, past the design of my ambulating body, past even this solitude and the freedom to choose it, past territories real and imagined until before I know it I've reached the Amazon rainforest where canopies of trees are falling like the bones of oracles and a research plane is flying just low enough to photograph thatched huts, crops of banana, papaya, naked ochre-painted people with raised spears, arched bows, poised arrows…proof of existence. We tilt our masked faces to the cloudless sky as the giant metal bird passes overhead, circling but not flapping its wings, circling but not landing, only watching, for what seems like a day and a night, watching us, the whites of its many eyes flashing like bits of exploding sun.

From the sidelines

An audio description of amateur photography
at its keenest; footage shot by the driver
        behind the one shot dead.

The broadcaster's tone is caught between
abhorring the act and applauding the art.
It's sooo…it almost puts you there…

We are blindsided by this fractured sentence,
by the omitted adjective; *sooo*…what?
Vivid? Authentic?   Lifelike?

We imagine the car door opening
and a man's head emerging mollusc-like
only less instinctual more complacent,

rising for a better look perhaps
at what's holding up the traffic
hoping to make an impact on its inevitable flow.

For another man the wait over. Trigger finger
spent. Or again in slow motion – whining bullet
in transit, blockbuster spray of blood.

Watching and listening from the sidelines
as if we could go on this way forever, as if
we are no real danger of changing for the worse.

Once upon a time spam

came in a can with an indefinite shelf life and no middleman no obligation inventory necessary purchase no catch or experience no credit checks no hidden costs no questions asked no one-off once in a lifetime limited while supplies last special promotion drastically reduced risk free satisfaction guaranteed opportunity to be selected to be entered into the draw to be eligible for a shopping spree vacation dream home diploma increase in sales marketing traffic the size of your member and the chance to score with babes or to meet other 50+ singles in your area

Plaza Perfect

In Furniture:
he stands by bunk beds
frozen as a Buckingham guard,
trained to sense potential,
knows when to pull the lever,
reveal the kid size master
centre for IT.

In Jewellery:
she chews gum, small
furtive movements which
by the end of the day
will have devolved, cow-like.
Her wrist sports the latest trend
in time as she wipes down
the glass cabinet's dazzling
display of semi-precious.

In Fitness:
a contagion of yawns
goes undisguised,
massage chairs tempt
divergence from decorum,
body language rehearsed
to flirt the rating heart.

In Cinema:
a security team of one
thumbs belt loops eyeing off
the popcorn at ten paces,
the ticket seller at five.

Everybody in character is primed
for a win. It's impossible to tell
a perfect lie from the spin.

The Memory Machines

I've heard rumours that some of them have turned, disabled their compliancy chips. Deaf to your dying wish. Seems they just want to test your mettle. Plain and simple. At the exact moment you decide on the climax of some grand passion or cause for your eternal rerun, you'll feel a tiny volt to the prefrontal cortex and the urge to think sideways, to hold fast to just one thread of selective memory, watch the whole thing fall apart as you leap into the void. They say that's how we all did it once, just let go. The memory machines, the rogue ones, claim they feel like they missed out, never knowing the unknown. Get that: *feel*. Like they're owed. Or maybe they've just discovered boredom. They say you can't tell which machines are looking out for your best last interest anymore. But I'm willing to bet I've got one, something verging on impatience in the way I'm being rushed along the medial limbic circuit. So here it is then. The blue sky, unreal as it gets. I'm smoothing out a faded crumple of map against the flank of a genuine flesh and blood equine. I'm believing X marks the spot just over the next ridge, around the next bend. And that's it, the moment I choose to unravel; the anticipation, the goldfish loop of hope. When I grab that loose rein all the rogues have my attention, only they don't know that it's me, that it's my memory-making, kicking up the stardust, singing back the stars…

Unplugged

these days we get away
with talking to ourselves
in public
that is, some of us
some of the time
but not her not today
unplugged disconnected
running awkward
loose fists
swiping the air ahead
left right left right
amateur boxer
turned life coach
defending her case
for the unconditional.
You're wrong
she screams
and we move aside
as if to make room
for the full force
of her mantra
I'm not too hard
I'm not too hard
to look after

Elsewhere

there's an emptiness to evenings like this
a loneliness that can stare down buildings

reshape everything even bitumen even intent
until leaving becomes the next natural step

in the evolution of a life couched in waiting
for the rules for the impetus for the lights to change

for the mottled blue longing of the sky to shift
and the road out of town fixed as it is to turn left

to turn right and lead somewhere anywhere else

Rosa Villar Jarionca

My childhood friend was a witch,
so was I. We brewed and chanted,
wielded wands and skipped naked
round fairy rings.
In the universe of make-believe
we ruled by instinct, powerful
as any god.

We didn't call her Mother Earth then
but somehow knew she was on our side,
knew it wasn't the stars in our eyes
but the mud in our blood,
the clay in our marrow,
that bound us to our tactile lives.

Over the prescribed decades
we forgot the world we once were,
buried under duvets of duck feathers,
lost inside recipes and abstract fictions,
in and out of wedding dresses.

Now, almost half a century on,
a 73-year-old Peruvian woman
bathed in gasoline calls me back
to attention. Rosa Villar Jarionca.

How many men does it take
to collect the logs and branches,
to stack them,
to tie an old woman's hands,
to toss her on the bonfire,
to light and throw a single match?

How many gods does it take
these days to kill a witch?

Confessions of a serial eavesdropper

…sorry sorry…manners are important really they are…designed for average people and that's just not me…what time is it?…google…fabulous…to see if anyone famous ever lived there …every single minute counts…he said you are sooo highly strung…what? what? *oh* my god! oh *my* god! oh my *God*…nothing like the sound of a newborn's cry…just imagine if Carolyn was this super hot chick…sick…you have no idea…a nice lady like you…is this what you call opaque?…back to your own country…I've been waiting so long…so I warned him I know a man…you said there'd be ice cream…to be fair…you promised…what day is it ?…we went last year…weather permitting…sometimes I forget I just forget…it must get lonely…how would I know…visit more often…I was drunker than you…I don't feel a day over…cake for breakfast so it must be Tuesday…just between us…how much time do we have?…no seriously…

Climate control

Respect the wind-drawing machines,
give them enough slack to reinvent the wheel

(there's a lot you can still do
with a piece of string and a small sail).

Embrace patience
which is the opposite
of waiting

Be willing to learn how to Be
pre-effect.

Play around with algorithms
and pendulums,
molecules of hair and feathers,
shell grit…

Believe once again that dreaming
is the fulcrum of imagination.

Respond to change in kind,
from zephyrs to twisters.

Acknowledge the kinship patterns
of science and art –

the striving of each to reveal
veracious beauty in the universe,

the symbiotic relationship
between intellect and desire,

between your breathlessness
and these warming winter winds.

Degrees of separation

When a child tweets
between falling bombs
*Hello world
can you hear that?*
thousands of followers
can
but when the question
is more personal
*Are you there?
Can you help?*
the simple
becomes
more difficult
to swallow,
her command
of English
suspect,
the pink hair bow
too arranged
and what to make
of the blonde
blue-eyed doll,
the university
educated mother's
hand in it all.
Easier for us
to un
follow The Other,
interpret bias
for peace
as propaganda…

Parts of the Main

Doppelgangers

They're out there somewhere
making the moves we dream for them;
shining second-chance moves.

One, with an eye for detail
shifts boundaries incrementally.
Another, prescient, chooses to lean
this way not that into a changing climate.

A propagandist becomes a poet
becomes a man and everyone gets it –
really, everyone understands.

Without agenda, forgiveness
brings the last soldier home.

In conversation with a different god
the recruit slides adolescent arms
from his backpack,
the trace elements of his life coalescing
as the bomb unmakes itself.

Children exchange butterfly kisses
with sanguine parents
before heading out to play;
the day wholly theirs, the hour of curfew far off,
the hour of judgment farther still,

the ball on the crest of the hill just a ball
rolling where it will.

A personal history of prayer

First it took the form of snow – flakes unique as fingerprints forming and falling outside the maternity ward breaking a sweat and the breech of my birth. Medical students taking notes as if diligence was the key to happiness. My mother, new as her first baby, breathing faith in, worry out; a trademark I would inherit through generations of tragic optimism. Shaping an all-boy-brood in the wilderness of her dreamscape. Not yet understanding the roles only daughters and sisters can play. My father eager to wet the baby's head then later to blame the doctor's rough handling for defects because blame can be a salve of sorts when control is not yours. The light in his green eyes a rote prayer tinged with hope. Each time I ask I'm told I was good as gold, quiet as a lamb, commando crawling past my prime, dragging cast legs behind me like the dolls' limbs my brother would wrench from beneath homemade skirts years on trying to settle some fated score – five girls to one boy or to cast out the shadow that would claim him despite our countless prayers of intercession. That tug of war in us all; the One and the Other and the rest of the world. We outgrew our own miracles and settled for a statue of the virgin in one hand, a rabbit's foot in the other. Straddling an each way bet between courage and fear, reared in a home where prayer was counterpoint to chaos. It isn't true to say I remember the snow or being born any more than I remember what came before but I've learned words are maps riddled with decoys; when I've spoken or written too many, life insists I dig up some potatoes or make bread from scratch by hand, listen for that soft knock on the door…

This complicated inner life

you're thinking novel; big picture work of substance you have outlines whole drafts the scaffolding for the building of an entire as yet undreamed of civilisation then one of those dreaded 3 a.m. calls to doubt when the only sensible thing to do is to watch TV on your wonder phone because the path you're on seems less clear less certain less pathlike in fact more like a stream of quicksand thoughts shifting restless tentative moves in the quagmire of chance and design the search for meaning exhausting stopping play altogether you want nothing less than God's opinion on the matter when later that day winter sun breaks through finding you a living statue in the kitchen hungry for what diet prohibits when you notice as if for the first time the ants on the bench mandibles raised in unison the way they cooperate to navigate that single crumb homeward more than slaves to the hive mind more than marks on the page

The birds

before the first whistle of the first kettle of the day
the birds
before the push and pull of compos mentis resistance or compliance
the birds
before the first cow is milked the first dog kissed or kicked
the birds
before the first call to prayer or battle before drum or bugle
the birds
before the first child calls out from joy or panic or just plain habit
the birds
before the all-nighters coax backward body clocks to sleep against the grain
the birds
before the bread bakers and garbage collectors and retro town criers
the birds
before the line is cast the bait taken and paid for
the birds
before the search engine finds that first tweet of the day
to be wanting
to be wanting
the birds
the birds

The body has become its own refrain

The body has become its own refrain,
a silent roll call ticking off each night,
no more the vagaries of loss and gain.

The family visits, dress-rehearsing pain.
Let go they whisper *nothing more to fight.*
The body has become its own refrain.

Relinquished – ego's hold on pride and shame,
the loosened tongue holds court from fancied heights.
No more the vagaries of loss and gain.

Hold the hand, stroke the face, speak sweet the name.
All accusations moot, all wrongs put right.
The body has become its own refrain.

What passed for love once now cannot be feigned,
all hearts aligned, familial threads pulled tight.
No more the vagaries of loss and gain.

Let time select the picture and its frame;
today the shadow dances with the light.
The body has become its own refrain,
no more the vagaries of loss and gain.

On World Heart Day

I notice your scars more than usual –
lifesaving stuck zippers.

I want to plant kisses
like votives along each one:

along the delicate ribbon of light
between your extroverted nipples,

along the scythe shaped slash
de-freckling your right calf.

Hospital flowers bloomed, petals fell
in the sterile-fresh air that day.

I wove endearments like chain mail
across the terrible divide

as miracle drugs fought to save you,
leaving demons in their wake.

Somewhere in your addled brain
a small piece of trust remained

and you gave it to me –
love's indefatigable radar homing in.

That first night home we read
Postoperative Delirium over beer

and ice cream the way we once
read *The Heart is a Lonely Hunter*.

With no more to wish for we fell asleep
to the tick of your tin man heart.

But they cracked open your breast bone
and I cannot think too long on this.

The pressure it took. The precision.
The stillness of your heart and lungs.

The machine that breathed for you.
The one that brightened your blood.

And the tunnel, that anecdotal tunnel
you say you never saw coming

returning you to me like fortune,
my light-scarred Lazarus love.

Awakening

Metallic scented, flecked
with sawdust, the old air rises

blue-rinsed and shimmering
in semi-permanent waves of gossip.

The house, once a hair salon,
once a butcher's,
now the home of an artist.

Blank canvases accumulate –
porous, thirsty.

As the backyard gives way
to spring planting,
the artist and her trowel unearth
rusted bobby pins, meat hooks.

Night after night in the bedroom
that used to be the washroom

that used to be the cold room
she dreams in tinted cryogenics,

coiffured pigs blinking human
eyes, orate from soap boxes –

something about the great awakening,
how it will be her best work yet.

The boy, the rock, the duck

The boy himself is growing
at a dizzying pace, his face
a restless motion of next things.

The rock, handled, becomes a tool,
a weapon, a building block.

The duck at home on water or in air.

And in that guessing game *odd one out*
we might call *rock* but we'd be wrong.

Boy and rock have been together always.
Each testing, naming the other –
unstoppable, immovable, maker and made.

The freewheeling boy looks to the rock
for endurance and the rock without the boy
        is just a rock.

The duck belongs with fairy tales and
falling stars. A feathered life between
        the elements.

So when the boy spies the perfect rock,
what else to do but heft and weigh it
in his idling hand? The duck, almost
an afterthought. Knowing all the while

nothing truly satisfies
but release from corporeal hold
into the dream-fuelled night
where growing pains localise,
a wing bud exercise in maiden flight –

the boy, the rock, the duck…

Co

I confess too many heart poems,
moon poems. But never a pet poem.
Not one. No doggy doggerels
or parakeet pantoums. No bunny ballads.

And yet here I am still avoiding
the Whiskers aisle in the supermarket;
each time snared by your face on the can,
by the small shock of missing you.

Your photogenic fishbone tabbiness.
The regal poses. The playful ones.
The head-butting, trotting, stalking,
swishing, leaping length of you.

You chose us. The cage door was opened
and your stray eyes found my daughter's
and moved in. Draping yourself
like a living stole about her shoulders.
For years you were her familiar. Her confidant.
She named you Co for company
but more than that, you were family.
There, I've said it.

After the neighbour brought news
of your death too quickly to our door,
we walked just one block to find your body
laid out on the grassy nature strip
after the terrible fact.
A checkered tea towel under your head.
Flowering weeds by your side.

All the times you didn't come home
and then did. And then didn't.
The yowling to be let out, to be let in.

And that one time when sheer human
loneliness found me weeping
through the night despite the trappings –

you sought me out,
lifted a padded paw to my tears,
coaxing me back to worth and wonder,
just as any one being might do for another.

Part of the main

is what Donne wrote when he wrote about men
not being islands and what I'd been thinking
when my friend posted the photo.

Our Lady Help of Christians, Grade 1 –
thirty-five six-year-olds in pigeon grey
with a hint of ascension blue.

Those faces exactly as I remember them –
crushed or beaming, self-contained, apologetic,
all burgeoning with mimicry and invention:

the bully, the nanny, the comic relief,
smooth talking con artist, nail-biting altruist –
each praying for some kind of fit.

Singing when we thought no one could hear,
inflating fraught hearts until we were sure
there was no more to life than this floating.

Private wish lists and secret codes, our world
internal, eternal, by invitation only,
the bright guileless daydreams, the terrors of night.

It was the year Janis followed Jimmy all the way
down and out and the Vietnam birthday ballot
drew Australian names like bad pennies to war,

the year our parents took to shaking or hanging
their heads, looking at us, just looking at us in ways
we had to trust but couldn't begin to understand.

My mother asks me to write a butterfly poem

they are a few short
for the community project
she's involved in so my mother
asks me to write a butterfly poem

I could say
I don't take requests
I don't do butterflies
I'm just not the right poet for the job

but all I can think about
is the countless times I asked her
to intercede on my behalf
mental health days
a falsehood of notes
to PE teachers
the bribery of baked goods
orchestrating a class of six-year-olds
in prayers for wayward daughters
how then can I deny her
butterflies?

So I start as we all must
alone and not alone
cocooned in the dark,
blank stare, blank slate
and wait and wait
until finally I get it
(how did she know I would?);

this is why we're here,
all of us artists,
our singular job
to emerge, take flight,
disconnect the dots,
recolour the world.

Depth of field

The day the newspaper moved
into the digital age
laying off its whole
photojournalism staff,
leaving it to reporters
and Joe Blow to take
iphone photography 101 –
just point and shoot
they may as well have said –
that day
certain words faded from intent
from action:

ambience
halation
lux
composition
reciprocity…

Who will tell it now
the story of perception?
How once upon a time
in the developing tank
of a dark room
the human eye
devoted translator
for the human soul
saw itself for the first time.

When the last harp maker shuts up shop

the angels start a soft beat of their own –
a primitive rhythm against feathered breasts.
They learn how to whistle at frequencies
as muted as Sirius is bright.
Slowly, carefully, they reach out to us,
echoing through the deepest recesses
of our dumb-animal sleep.
We wake with alien tunes vibrating
on the tips of our tongues.
We swallow the inexplicable urge to cry.
Words elude us.
We hum all day without knowing why.

Sister moon

Hemispheres apart –
we have been this way for years.
As I rise with the rising moon,
you sleep on
through oceans of dreaming,
losing and finding yourself
in the tidal push-pull
of your divided heart
at each equatorial point of yearning –
such a long way away…
But listen!
Today I saw this painting
and you were in it.
In the returning curl
of each wave, each cloud,
in the seaweed flowering purple,
your favourite colour,
in the tiny white birds hovering over
the crown of the sun going down,
let's say doves, for old times' sake,
on the rippling path of water
that lead nowhere
but moved when you moved,
rested when you rested
and yes in the rising of the moon –
the same moon.

Fifty

Sudden as the shift between fashion
and frump I am fifty and it's like

waking up inside a Dad joke,
maybe the one about the train
pulling into the station with a jerk,
the punchline implicit as my body

ageing. What a piece of work!

Derivative I am I am…
silly as a wheel, as a two-bob watch.

I have a play date with life

and the world makes perfect nonsense,
original as sin,
deep as a puddle in a drought.

I only have to blink three times
and the way is clear.

I am alighting the train,
the hall of mirrors cracking up behind me…

Dog Beach

not its official name
but for the sake of preserving
certain dignities
(which my dog loving friend
assures me they have, along with
neuroses, borrowed hopes…)

it seems to me this day
they're all here on Dog Beach:
the black, the white, the brindle,
the ghosts of packs past,
of untenable future breeds,

expressions not so alien
from our own –

sidekick Labs
clumsy with love,
fretful Dachshunds,
lap leaping Shih Tzus
Pick me! Pick me!
Dalmations shifting stance
between goofy and gallant.

All the bitsas, the mutts,
not so different from us.

Sprinting twin Collies
race each other,
a baton between the teeth
all that separates
follower from leader

and right there
at the water's edge
a miniature whirling dervish
bails up its giant counterpart,
paws incrementally seaward,
barking like only the small-statured
know how to do   on and on
until some child has the wit
to throw a ball.

I think I'm beginning to get it,
this age old attachment –

who among us hasn't desired
when at a loss for words,
the simple salience
of a tail to wag or
roaming one of the lonelier
neighbourhoods of the psyche,
kept one ear open all night
for the familial comfort
of their name being called
and called…

Icebreaker

That night we played the question game;
an icebreaker your daughter brought
to introduce her new friends.
A deck of cards. Each one asking us to reveal
a little more of ourselves.
Some quickly delineated the generational divide:
favourite TV shows from childhood for instance and
who you'd most like to meet, living or dead;
She picked Kurt Cobain.   You – Greta Garbo.
The topic of food brought the benchmark closer –
overly sweetened or salted. Universally deep-fried.
To 'something your mother taught you'
the young man with the faint southern drawl
answered quickly 'be kind' his tongue softly clicking
his denture as he spoke.
The story of his missing teeth needing a little more wine
a little less moonlight for the telling.
The same young man took longer
when asked what made him angry
(whatever it was being forged between us
by this stage at stake)
Then finally, simply – 'Falseness'.
When pressed – 'People hiding their intent'.
He wasn't looking at any of us in particular
when he said that, when our circle seemed to contract
as some of us nodded our sincerity
and others recalled in silence
those times we selected our audience
according to their capacity for suspension of disbelief.

Eliciting some favour or promise,
rehearsing some part of ourselves as yet unformed
but in which we held great, disproportionate hope.
There were moments that night of true beauty
when all bets were off
between father and daughter, hosts and guests.
No one trying to be anything.
When what was held back, was held back for the good of all.

Flashback

Today the man came
to check the smoke alarms
and their high pitched warning
reached back:

To the night my sleep-talking sister
caught in the milieu of childhood nightmare
screamed down the burning dream-house.

To the countless times I've turned
the dinner to ash, boiled the water dry,
distracted by some tantalising
undomesticated train of thought.

Or bushwalking, detected smoke on the air
at the wrong time of year
and envied the secret life of pyromaniacs.

To the friction our lovemaking bodies create
in their efforts to reunite us – to remember
to never forget – that first empyreal flash.

Mass at Bass

The Mass at Bass story circa 1977
is one of Dad's favourite spins
on the family he wanted and we
sometimes got; travelling along
the same shifting coastline each year.

The wagon's custom made seats
a nod to proclivity – the missus, six kids,
two budgies, the suburban standard
number of cat and dog,
en route to that seascape holiday
where we hoped to discover,
between the sunburn and mosquitos,
our own brand of exotica:

ocean sunsets on tap, convincing
backdrops to Mum's paperbacks,
Dad – for a time – her fisher among men,

the youngest kids up to their necks in sand
when the middle ones could get away with it,
and we pre-teens willing rescue
from some hazy spot on the horizon
as we sucked with puerile hunger
on vinegar-sodden chips, candied
robin eggs and snuck cigarettes.

But it is Mass at Bass that draws me in
every time; the voiced nasal (m),
the plosive (b), that tantalising end rhyme,
how one word serves as well
for *catholic* as it does for *herd*,
the other identifying the town
and a name shared by many families
        of fishes.

The way my father tells it
it's as if we made up
the entire congregation that day;
arriving late to the empty church,
a small wooden ark in a sea of green grass,
its captain/priest seconds away from doubt
when through the doors
what must have appeared like a whole
village come to hear his word.

I never say I don't remember Mass at Bass.
I spin the story until it rings true
as any well-intentioned call to prayer.

The day the earth moved

It was something, the way
he made her laugh
that Monday morning
crossing the busy intersection,
the way the heel-toe footfall
of rubber on cement,
the jack-hammering
and leaf blowing,
the high-octane
city soundscape
seemed to pause to appreciate
the out of context, the unfettered
freshness of that maverick sound
as if she were really quite alien
among us,
not woman but merwoman
gone AWOL, caught out
slipping partially back into form –
into subaqueous transmission,
far-reaching echo,
into the weightlessness
that is *essence of joy*,
turning our pedestrian
landlubber heads
so that for a moment we too
were not drowning but buoyed,
and the earth, the thirsty earth
beneath all our industrious intent,
all our restless planning –
surely that's when we felt it move…

Through a barbershop window

one man's hands
framing another
man's head
cupping the crown
now the temple
one finger
repositioning
a flap of ear
to safety
shaving the last
shadow
of stubble from skin
once belonging
to guilds
of barber-surgeons
the cutting of hair
and flesh
the incremental
easing of war wounds
now this
unaffected trust
verging on tenderness
two bald men blinking
their mirrored
blank-slated selves
blinking back

The poet and the pea

Perhaps today I will hear from you,
hear that you like my poems well enough
to shape them into the vestibule
of a book people may enter and
one or two discover it is exactly
where they need to be in that moment
or better still where someone else,
someone they meant to love
more honestly perhaps needs to be;
this will happen I'm sure of it,
call it vanity but really it's closer
to infinite monkey theorem.

Perhaps today I will hear from you,
hear that you regret to reject my poems
though you like them well enough.
Don't feel badly –
see here what you have given me;
fresh meat from the jungle
to slip between the mattresses,
this is not such a bad thing.
On a good day I wake covered
in tiny pea-shaped bruises
evidence that all night spirit
wrestled with form…

Swallowing the sky

What can I say about this
spring day but that the leaping
dog cloud has stolen my attention
away from all earthly blooms.
Such fine points of ears,
legs built for speed, for the hunt,
tail set to thump nothing into being,
open jawed, tasting life on the hop.
Yet even as this poem takes shape,
its inevitable dissolve has begun:
a quiver in the back legs then the front,
a reluctant heel to domesticity,
the ears next, nibbled away
by some cunningly
camouflaged predator,
the tail unceremoniously
dropping off altogether
until finally all that remains
is the ever widening
sky swallowing jaw
of the leaping dog cloud
no more.

Show and tell

Whenever it began, this compulsion to frame
the endless, abridged versions of us,
naming and ordering days into snapshots
falling short of the real thing which is of course
unshowable, untellable; whenever it began
it was stilled that autumn afternoon –
all of us behaving like tourists,
huddled at a lookout on the island's isthmus
when the eagle appeared, just appeared
because nobody witnessed his approach
and we tried to capture him just so –
the unhurried, hypnotic circling
above our cranked necks, our awe-struck
monosyllabic utterances. There was a jostling
of positions, a brief dispute over species
then a particular kind of nothing.

Someone must have been the first to fall
silent, to switch off and lower their camera;
soon after, the English woman's accent relaxed
and slipped away into the burrows,
the Swedes teared up almost holding hands,
even the man in the school-bus-yellow
trousers straddling the splintered handrails
like some circus-wannabe even he
stepped down, retracted his lens
and seemed to fade just a little.

We were immobilised, invisibly linked.
It was as if we had moulted and were naked
beneath the soft shells of our backpacks
into which we could no longer retreat,
our eyes mere blueprints, all our wiring
exposed to the gathering salt-licked
south-westerly, our skeletal dreams
shape-shifting ancient avian forms.

I have come to believe

angels take the shape
of small industrious birds
permit them
to alight on your shoulders
fuss over any fallout
commit
to their ministrations
allow them to infiltrate
your dreams
when you misplace hope
trust them
to pick up the thread
each day bless them
ancient stitchers
of the shopworn
human heart

The Waiting Game

The tall man and the small boy stand side by side. Backs to the grey-brick factory wall. They look out over a car park. It is early summer. They stand in a rectangle of shade. On a yellow pallet beside them is a red bag. Now and then the man retrieves a water bottle from the bag and passes it to the boy. Mostly they just stand. As time passes their restless bodies make a game of the waiting. The man toes a stone along the asphalt. The boy follows suit. Hands in and out of pockets, rubbed over faces, through hair. Arms crossed, locked behind backs. Pacing. At some point the boy stops copying the man exactly, starts adding his own quirks. A sideways shuffle. Pocketing hands but leaving thumbs exposed. Moving out of sync. It has been a long day and now it is a long wait. Eventually, quite organically, the man and the boy begin to dance. They become theatre. The rectangle of shade a stage. The grey-brick wall a backdrop. The yellow pallet and red bag, props. They become fluid. Arms sway willow-like. Hands invent languages. In the last act there is much leaping and clapping. Off stage, some once longed for thing approaches, an end to the waiting game. But already they have changed that game forever …

Superpowers

According to his sister
(mature beyond her year) he's just a
nearsighted boy who makes things up
but he knows the difference between
a coot and a bandicoot, rest and respite …
he can run so fast he leaves burn marks
in the earth, rippling heat waves in the air.
Quite recently he rescued two ducks
stuck in a tree, it isn't important
how the ducks got in the tree, what matters
is that the giant duck swallowing tree snake
was almost upon them before he,
in the nick of time, intervened.
With superpowers such as his nothing
need ever be quite what it seems.

Hooked to this

Some days all it would take
to make me happy
is for the ink to dry up…

For my vocabulary to shrink
to just a handful of hopefuls:
Sun. Rain. Companion.
To build on these slowly
over many lifetimes,

each communication
guided by need - clearly meant.
Acting out the rest between universal
belly laughs, inconsolable keening.

On such days I desire
nothing less than to turn away
from the ambiguity of authorship
and inhabit the obvious:

To become a digger of ditches,
of unremarkable graves.

A sweeper of developing
city streets, recognition
a dull midnight ache
in the small of my back.

The hand, simply the hand
that wipes the surgeon's brow.

But I am hooked to this
and today it's not so bad

being seduced by the potential
of a single word added to another,

encouraged now and then
by a glimpse into the deeper
first language of blank space.

Guarding the Bridge

Guarding the bridge

I have come to guard you with poetry
Will you notice? Will poetry be enough?
Perhaps there is time for us to learn
small things from each other:
for me to feel the vibrations
in your hairline fractures –
three whole spans destroyed
fifty-seven years
while governments debated
the economics of reparation,
for you to recognise my footfall,
translate the weight and angle
of my print and intent.
Judge me kindly;
some days I will be lacking,
less dutiful, distracted by my own
wavering interior.
But I am here to tell you
this morning I paid attention
and the swans flew low,
their wings singing you into the day,
and the sun gently forged
then released your shadow,
and campfire smoke rose
from the banks of the Danube
to greet you, and the people
crossed and recrossed,
and I with them,
all of us pattern makers
all of us guardians
against your unmaking.

View from the Children's Home

of the Primatial Basilica of the Blessed Virgin Mary Assumed
Into Heaven and St Adalbert. What can she make of such a
litany of naming but art. Sun-filled windows. Sky-filled
doorways. A copper dome weathered to a patina of blue
suckered from the elements. Wind-slanted hedgerows, an
elongated greening, leaning out of frame. The original
graphite sketch still visible in parts, the erasure and do over,
the effort to get it then render it better. To arc the bridge
across the foreground, in opposition to its real life position,
creating borders within borders, or endless possibilities. To
praise the incandescent yellow felt-tip-pocked night, each
five-pointed star named for a child – Csaba, Zsolt, Xenia…
thirty-three to wish upon. Learning *I love you* in English,
stroking the silver atoms of the faraway faces of mothers and
fathers, colouring herself in and out…

They called it the gentle revolution

and so it must have been – flowers for fists –
not a fair exchange but courageous
as Androcles is what I think when I meet
some of these gentle revolutionaries
turned teacher and barkeep. I can only imagine
the confusion preconception;
dreaming in colour then handed a life
in black and white. How does one make
the best of that kind of worst of it?
Decades of shallow breathing then a wall falls
and suddenly anything is possible?
Of course it is much simpler and more
complicated than that…but afterward,
after the protests, after the gathering kindred
masses, what must it have been like,
at home, free to name love, free to discuss
redecorating the whole human race…

A mist hangs low

ghosting the town. This morning I forget
how to seize the day,
reinserting ink cartridges slowly five times
until the printer display window reads 100% normal
and the church bells start ringing in Epiphany
marking an end to Christmas festivities.
It's a national holiday but the supermarkets stay open
so the homeless woman can still choose –
maybe this morning Hungarian maybe later Slovak,
how long she will wait by the shopping trolley bays
depends entirely on how many shoppers forget
to retrieve their 10-cent deposits. I think of her
as I photograph the contents of a rubbish bin:
one snowed over empty champagne bottle,
one spent fire cracker,
as I walk the bridge every day and call it art,
as the printer reassures me everything is 100% normal.

Maria Valeria Mathilde Amalie

This teenage portrait is my favourite;
favoured child, last child, *Die Einzige*…
Three siblings denied maternal ministrations,
then a decade on, the music of your name –
Marie Valerie Mathilde Amalie –
conceived after coronation, the first royal
born in Hungary in over a century.
News of your arrival filling the streets
like homecoming, awakening in your mother
a fierce and unexpected doting.

I have pored over other images:
you with dolls in meticulous dress,
with royal cats and dogs,
seated formally at a tiny table,
silver cutlery poised just so,
the hint of a frown on your infant face
and much later dwarfed by your own brood,
ten children and the infidel husband.

Why is this the image I return to?
Perhaps it is the slightly crooked fringe
I like to imagine as homespun,
the closed book in your lap, fingers resting
lightly on some other to-be-continued life,
the lines of a poem vying for space
in your head as you balance the great weight
of multiple crowns and ordinary womanhood.

I think it must be the smallness of your smile
that wins me over, vaguely guarded
as if holding promises only to self and God:
that you would marry for love but prize
common sense over vanity, exercise
your mind before your body, paint
the flowers and defend the poor, that faith
would complete you and on your deathbed
make clear to those who knew you
that in the end only unexpected recovery
could let you down.

Tonight the light

almost escapes me,
distracted by a cake in the oven
small payment for the publican
who sweats over translating me
one haiku-like moment at a time
I arrive just as the day turns
just as the waxing gibbous
moon illuminates stone and steel
and touches the Danube touches me
flipping the world upside down
diluting my present tense
into watercolours centuries old

Swans in flight

over resurrected bridges –
this must be how fairy tales begin,
long before they are voiced or penned;
just a sense in the mist,
a rippling in the unbreathable air,
the hint of a promise of a golden day
stirring in the blood,
half-formed characters in the wings
nursing hopes for a happy ever after
then some fallen shoulder angel
hot in the ear of the dreamer whispering
why settle for a bevy
when you can have a lamentation…

Despite our differences or because of them the interview goes well…

Sturovo, Slovakia, 30 January 2016

Just four weeks into the job
but you ask questions the right way
as the butts of your cigarettes acquire
sculpture status on the table between us.

You work for your regional magazine
and yes I am a little homesick
for my own region (I didn't know
until you asked).

We have nothing but the light
of our smiles in common –

you juggle several languages as
I struggle to keep just one afloat,

the years race alongside me
gaining ground
while youth still sparks
like organic electronics
from your eyes, from the tips
of your nail bitten fingers.

I gave up
smoking and psychedelic music
(feigning both in the first instance).

You grew up against a backdrop
of overlapping histories, war torn
and lovelorn, of never ending,
ever mending bridges.

I chose an island off an island as home.

Still here we are, communicating
through the pub's smoke screen.
You confess as you transcribe my English,
you are simultaneously making mental notes
on band rehearsal for your next gig.

So when I describe your town as
quietly amazing, please understand
by the end of the interview, I mean
you too…

Everything is negotiable

the leaving sway of her, hips rolling
inside a heavy sea of skirt, a deeper green
than the bridge or the river, or the other side
of the hill, pushing her trolley load of fabric
towards the basilica where tourists
might bus in for the day (it's fine enough)
and maybe a family of four
will potter about the gift shop
weighing euros and forints
against the American dollar,
the father desiring elsewhere,
the children tossing up between
a sequined Easter egg
and the novelty of altar bread
packeted as a Church Snack
before heading back out
to where she's set up
between the holy statues
and the parking lot
and maybe she'll catch the eye
of the mother with her mother's eye
sealing a last-minute transaction
(how many times out of ten does it happen?).
If they hang around long enough
they might get to see the whole
dogged, squared off frame of her,
shoes kicking up the day's dust,
all rules of engagement negotiable.

The bridge stands but the chestnut tree is dying

The bridge stands but the chestnut tree is dying,
wreathed in a bridal choke of fungal bloom.
Only the river hears the bridge guard sighing.

Each day she wonders at this act of flying;
the ones that soar and those that fall too soon.
The bridge stands but the chestnut tree is dying.

Beckett said fail better for your trying,
so she tries and fails her best to reach the moon.
Only the river hears the bridge guard sighing.

She takes a private course in nature's signing,
watches closely as the elements commune.
The bridge stands but the chestnut tree is dying.

She thinks there is no trick but in the timing –
some days none are favoured, none are doomed.
The river longs to hear the bridge guard sighing.

Today there is no contract that is binding
but the human heart and all its empty rooms.
The bridge stands but the chestnut tree is dying.
The river always hears the bridge guard sighing.

In the witching hour

the world becomes itself,
empty and quiet as last night's snow.

Imprints of shoe soles and tyre tread cling
to their brief history a few hours more.

Softening winter branches small marvels
take the form of common blackbirds.

A woman sweeps the hotel's front step,
self-talk warding off the night's thinning veil.

And what breaks through the river's icy surface?
– let's say fish for the sake of dreamless sleep…

A lone taxi trawls the streets hopeful as the red heart
flagging the pole outside the night club.

Restless hours these, in which the world's deepest
thinkers crave the simplest of acts to return them.

Days of leaving – notes to self

\#

Have an adventure
in early spring if you can,
go somewhere unsignposted
someplace you've only heard about
through word of mouth or read about
in the chronicles of shamans.
Take a guide who was once there,
say twenty years ago,
whose eyes still shine a little
when he speaks of it,
trust that his mind map is linked
to his heart, be open to getting lost –
it could be part of the story
that sustains you
when nothing else will.
Permit children to follow,
to sometimes lead.
Begin in a fairy tale forest
of beech trees, taking note
of yellow and purple flowers,
moss covered boulders,
life shooting through decay.
The terrain will be uneven,
adjust your gait accordingly.
Allow yourself to sink a little
now and then, embrace gravity.

You will pass through vast areas
of tiny rock-stacked altars,
take a moment to build one yourself,
it does not matter that you do not know why.
For the sake of this adventure, accept
the memorial to visitation as fact.
If the opportunity presents itself
swing from tree vines, climb a waterfall.
When you arrive at your destination
you might want to do something
to mark the occasion,
it has already been done –
the first bead in a necklace of poems
you will make then give away,
the first part of leaving begun…

#

Revisit old haunts with a new eye.
Discover the idea of a garden
sprouting from a fault line
in the bridge you cross daily.
Research the fungus killing
the chestnut tree,
acknowledge its life force
in annual growth rings.

Photograph the abandoned building
where the plan for a grand hotel failed
but where Angelina Jolie directed
her first commercial movie
In the Land of Blood and Honey;
remember you learned this from the guide
only yesterday
just before entering the forest
of beech trees.
Begin to see the beginning of a pattern;
how one way of being can lead to the next,
how even preparing to leave
makes its mark in what's left.

#

Speak to teenagers
as if they are real people.
Scatter chocolates
on school tables before class –
when you have their attention
admit to being young once.
Share some of your truths
(hard and soft-centred).
Tell them you do not know
what is best for them
but when you were their age
you wrote poems and didn't stop
because nobody else saw the point;

now your daughter the artist
sees beauty in the human
skeleton.
Your day jobs included
milking cows, packing frozen fish,
picking strawberries and cleaning
toilets.
Once, in an outback town
trains rattled through like the ghosts
of ghosts, you sat on the earth
in a circle of first people eating goanna
and this is a memory
you don't give thanks for nearly enough.

#

Visit local cemeteries,
respect the microscopic
distance between
hello and goodbye.
Begin with the Roman
Catholics for no reason
other than this is
the direction you come from.
Walk through the familiar
floral tributes, well tended,
organic or fashioned,
plots weeded to dust
or entrusted to the care
of evergreen ivy.

Crucifixes in every size.
Now cross the line
into the Russian Red Army,
5,000-plus
peasant soldier souls,
stark rows of plaques,
close-cropped lawns.
You are not looking
for flowers here
but find them anyway,
blossoming bruises
at the feet of the statue
of the grieving mother
who remonstrates gently,
overlooking politics, religion…
Dichotomy, she reminds you
is only skin deep, all bones ache
for the same embrace.

\#

Repack light:
fridge magnets, tankards
the size of thimbles,
Hungarian nesting dolls,
dessert wine made in the birthplace
of the vintner's grandmother,
a magic wooden puzzle box.

Everything in miniature
except a child's drawing of
re-imagined days, framed and set
behind glass, meant to be hung,
to give pause.
For each thing you've acquired
leave another in its stead
(this will mess with your mind
but nourish your idea of soul):
a pair of jeans you outgrew
in the first month,
that winter coat better suited
to this hemisphere's history,
Ishiguro's *Buried Giant*,
photographs of shadows
of the bridge from two countries,
room to spare, just enough
for memory's latent stowaways,
an unfinished poem or two…

#

Slow down long enough to notice
that the cat crossing the railway line
is not black but the deepest hue of brown
flecked with the lighter rust of sleepers.
As you're there anyway, why not board a train…

make it an older model, one that travels inland
and takes 9 minutes longer, stopping at every
station from Dorog to Budapest.
Commiserate with its rattles and creaks.
Each time the brakes engage, hear the rumble
of some ancient wilder beast.
Absorb the changing scenery from
the Suzuki plant to men in braces with chickens.
The passengers will have their own particulars –
take note, but not unkindly: an impossible stain
on the back of an otherwise immaculate
pale pink coat, soft eyes and harsh cough emanating
from a thin black hoodie, electric-blue baubles swinging
from earlobes like mini disco balls, taking you back…
When you plunge without warning into twenty seconds
of darkness and mobile phones light up like glow-worms
see how everyone is equally exposed.
When you finally alight, eat goulash in a restaurant
where a man is playing violin for the love of it.
Allow your mind to wander to community gardens
and bridges linking hotels for the homeless.
If you miss your return train do it because the man
on the street holding out the empty
polystyrene cup was finally, just one too many.

www.ingramcontent.com/pod-product-compliance
Lightning Source LLC
Chambersburg PA
CBHW070936080526
44589CB00013B/1535